Greek-English Dictionary for Kids

A simple picture dictionary for English-speaking children who are learning to read Greek

Over 350 words and phrases
Pronunciation guide included

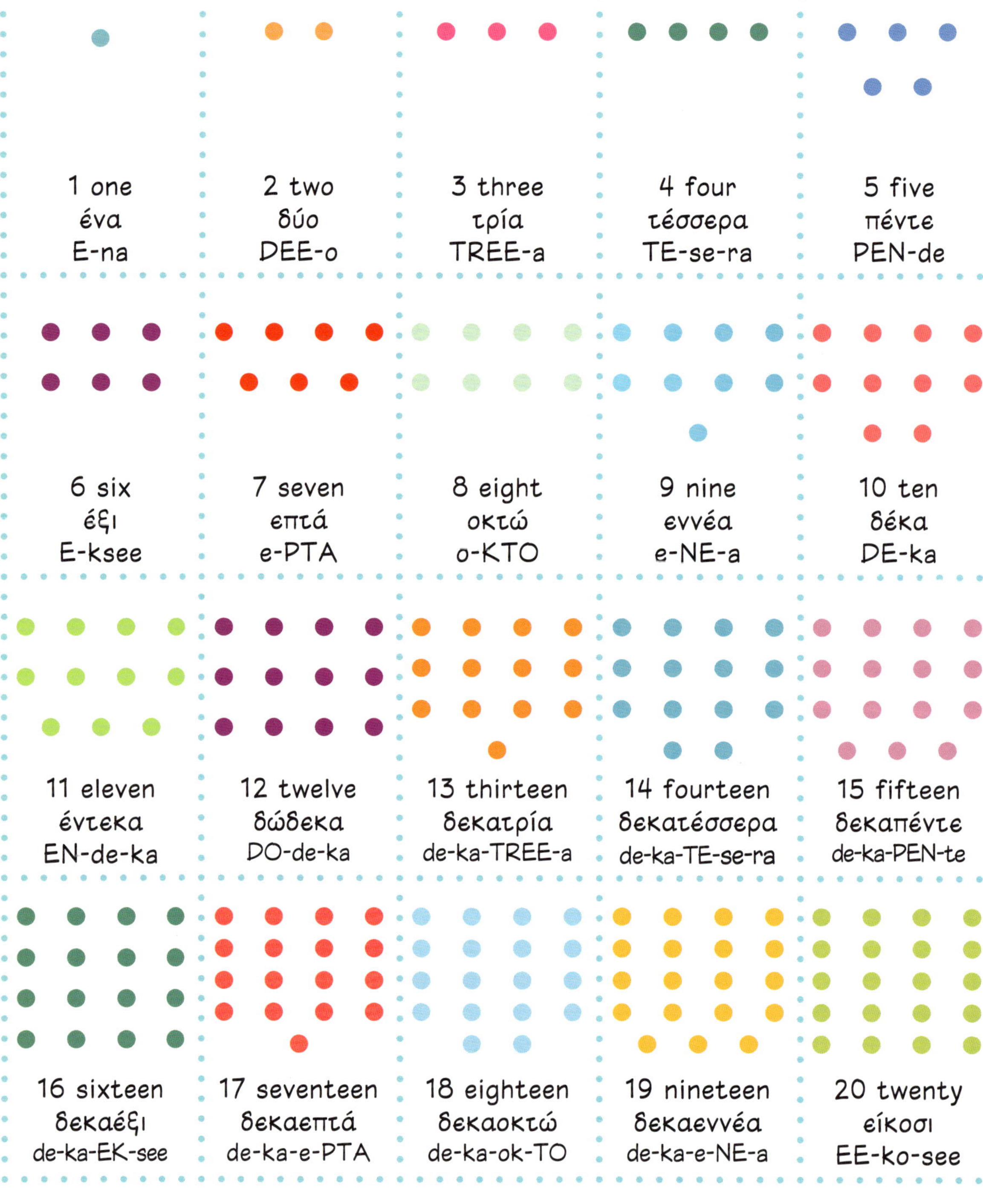
1 one
ένα
E-na
2 two
δύο
DEE-o
3 three
τρία
TREE-a
4 four
τέσσερα
TE-se-ra
5 five
πέντε
PEN-de
6 six
έξι
E-ksee
7 seven
επτά
e-PTA
8 eight
οκτώ
o-KTO
9 nine
εννέα
e-NE-a
10 ten
δέκα
DE-ka
11 eleven
έντεκα
EN-de-ka
12 twelve
δώδεκα
DO-de-ka
13 thirteen
δεκατρία
de-ka-TREE-a
14 fourteen
δεκατέσσερα
de-ka-TE-se-ra
15 fifteen
δεκαπέντε
de-ka-PEN-te
16 sixteen
δεκαέξι
de-ka-EK-see
17 seventeen
δεκαεπτά
de-ka-e-PTA
18 eighteen
δεκαοκτώ
de-ka-ok-TO
19 nineteen
δεκαεννέα
de-ka-e-NE-a
20 twenty
είκοσι
EE-ko-see

Index - Περιεχόμενα

A WORD ABOUT OUR PRONUNCIATION GUIDE

Each dictionary entry includes a guide with English letters to show how Greek words are pronounced. Greek words have accents, to reflect that capital letters are used in the accented syllable. Some Greek sounds can not be replicated exactly in English. Please refer to the guide below to help you pronounce the words correctly.

- When you see an "α" in this guide, it is pronounced in Greek as "ah" or "aa", as in the word "father".
- The letter, "β", is pronounced like the English letter, "v", as in the word "vote."
- The Greek "γ" has a soft "g" sound. It does not sound like the "g" in the word "gate", for example. It's a soft, gutteral "g" from the back of the throat, that almost sounds like a "y", in the word "yes." For simplicity, we use the letter "g" in the guide in most cases, except when it sounds like an English "y". In those cases, we use the letter "y".
- The Greek "δ" has a soft sound, closer to the "th" in the English word "the" or "then." For simplicity, we use the English letter, "d" in the guide to indicate this. However, we also use the letter "d" to reflect the sound made whenever a Greek word includes the following two letters: "ντ".
- An "ε" in this guide is pronounced in Greek like the "e" in the word "elephant."
- When an "ee" is used in the guide, it is pronounced in Greek like the "e"-sound in the words "read" or "weed."
- the Greek, "θ", is pronounced like the English "th" as in the word "think".
- the Greek "μπ" is pronounced like an English "b".
- the Greek "x" is pronounced like an English "h".
- the Greek "σx" combines an "s" and a hard "h" in English, not the "shhh" sound that we get in English. To reflect that, we use "s(ho)" to indicate that you need to pronounce both the "s" and the "h" separately.

The family - Η οικογένεια

ee ee-ko-YE-nee-a

mother/Mom
η μητέρα/η μαμά
ee mee-TE-ra/ee ma-MA

father/Dad
ο πατέρας/ο μπαμπάς
o pa-TE-ras/o ba-BAS

grandfather
ο παππούς
o pa-POOS

grandmother
η γιαγιά
ee ya-YA

sister
η αδερφή
ee a-der-FEE

brother
ο αδερφός
o a-der-FOs

cousins
τα ξαδέρφια
ta ksa-DER-fya

aunt
η θεία
ee THEE-a

uncle
ο θείος
o THEE-os

The house - Το σπίτι

to SPEE-tee

bedroom
το υπνοδωμάτιο
to ee-pno-do-MA-tee-o

living room
το καθιστικό
to ka-thee-stee-KO

garden
ο κήπος
o KEE-pos

kitchen
η κουζίνα
ee koo-ZEE-na

bathroom
το μπάνιο
to BA-nyo

toilet
η τουαλέτα
ee too-a-LE-ta

ceiling
το ταβάνι
to ta-VA-nee

floor
το πάτωμα
to PA-to-ma

staircase
η σκάλα
ee SKA-la

In the house - Μέσα στο σπίτι

ME-sa sto SPEE-tee

sofa
ο καναπές
o ka-na-PES

armchair
η πολυθρόνα
ee po-lee-THRO-na

curtains
οι κουρτίνες
ee koor-TEE-nes

cushion
το μαξιλαράκι
to ma-ksee-la-RA-kee

television
η τηλεόραση
ee tee-lee-O-ra-see

table
το τραπέζι
to tra-PE-zee

stool
το σκαμνάκι
to ska-MNA-kee

computer
ο υπολογιστής
o ee-po-lo-yee-STEES

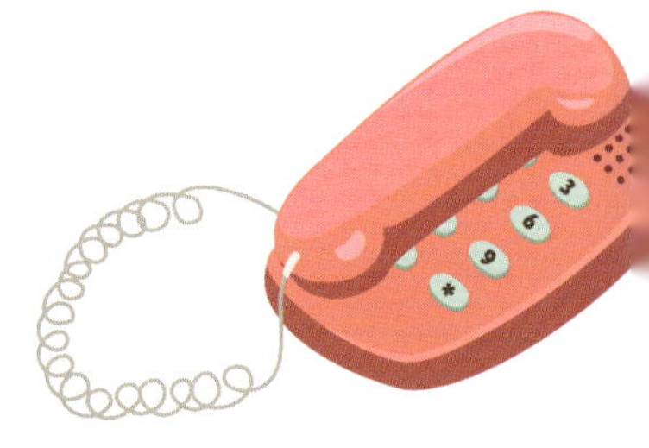

telephone
το τηλέφωνο
to tee-LE-fono

The bedroom - Η κρεβατοκάμαρα

EE kre-va-to-KA-ma-ra

bed
το κρεβάτι
to kre-VA-tee

chest of drawers
το κομοδίνο
to ko-mo-DEE-no

wardrobe
η ντουλάπα
ee doo-LA-pa

rug
το χαλάκι
to ha-LA-kee

window
το παράθυρο
to pa-RA-thee-ro

shelf
το ράφι
to RA-fee

alarm clock
το ξυπνητήρι
to ksee-pnee-TEE-ree

door
η πόρτα
ee POR-ta

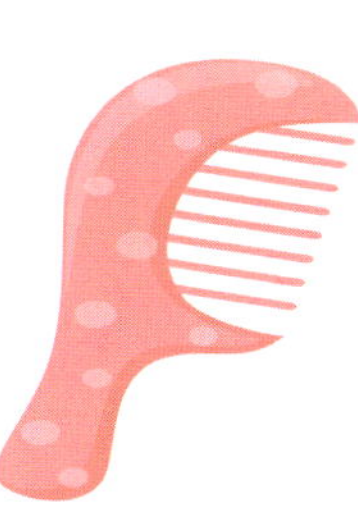

comb
η χτένα
ee HTE-na

The bathroom - Το μπάνιο

to BA-nyo

washbowl
ο νιπτήρας
o nee-PTEE-ras

toilet
η τουαλέτα
ee too-a-LE-ta

bathtub
η μπανιέρα
ee ba-NYE-ra

mirror
ο καθρέφτης
o ka-THRE-ftees

towel
η πετσέτα
ee pe-TSE-ta

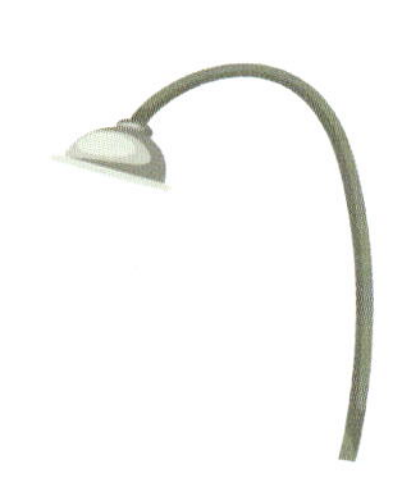

shower
το ντους
to DOOS

soap
το σαπούνι
to sa-POO-nee

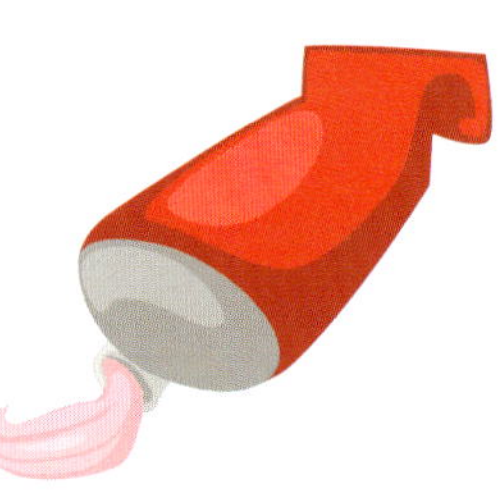

toothpaste
η οδοντόπαστα
ee o-don-DO-pa-sta

toothbrush
η οδοντόβουρτσα
ee o-don-DO-voor-tsa

The kitchen - Η κουζίνα

ee koo-ZEE-na

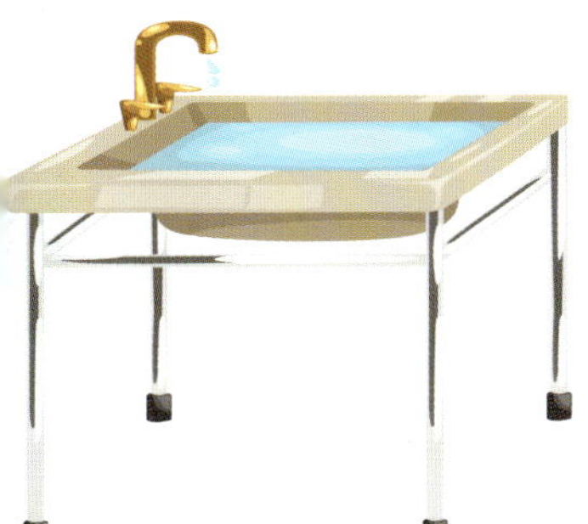

sink
ο νεροχύτης
o ne-ro-HEE-tees

stove
ο φούρνος
o FOOR-nos

refrigerator
το ψυγείο
to psee-YEE-o

pot
η κατσαρόλα
ee ka-tsa-RO-la

glass
το ποτήρι
to po-TEE-ree

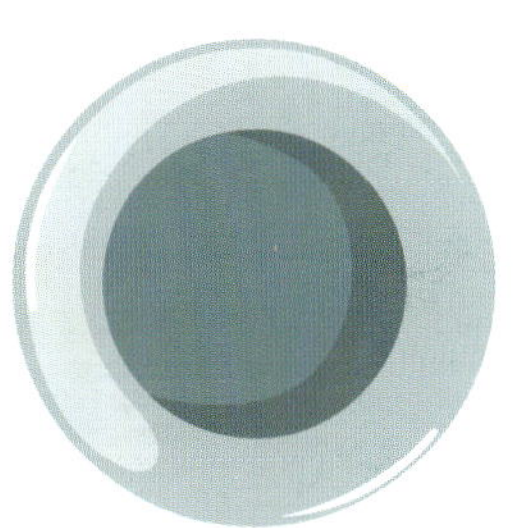

plate
το πιάτο
to PYA-to

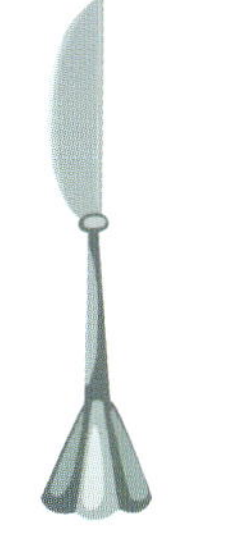

knife
το μαχαίρι
to ma-HE-ree

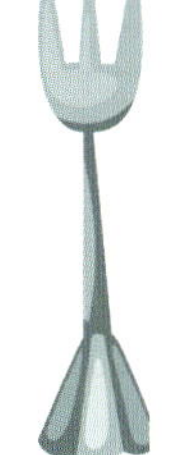

fork
το πιρούνι
to pee-ROO-nee

spoon
το κουτάλι
to koo-TA-lee

The body - Το σώμα

to SO-ma

head
το κεφάλι
to ke-FA-lee

eyes
τα μάτια
ta MA-tya

nose
η μύτη
ee MEE-tee

mouth
το στόμα
to STO-ma

shoulders
οι ώμοι
ee O-mee

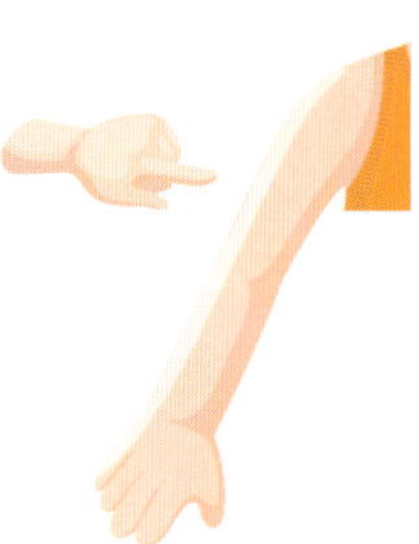

arm
το μπράτσο
to BRA-tso

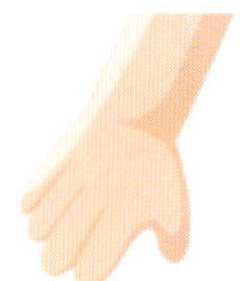

hand
το χέρι
to HE-ree

leg
το πόδι
to PO-dee

knee
το γόνατο
to GO-na-to

Clothes - Τα ρούχα

ta ROO-ha

skirt
η φούστα
ee FOO-sta

pants
το παντελόνι
to pan-te-LO-nee

shirt
το πουκάμισο
to pou-KA-mee-so

dress
το φόρεμα
to FO-re-ma

coat
το παλτό
to pal-TO

pajamas
οι πιτζάμες
ee pee-TZA-mes

shoes
τα παπούτσια
ta pa-POO-tsya

socks
οι κάλτσες
ee KAL-tses

hat
το καπέλο
to ka-PE-lo

The city - Η πόλη

ee PO-lee

house
το σπίτι
to SPEE-tee

school
το σχολείο
to s(h)o-LEE-o

post office
το ταχυδρομείο
to ta-hee-dro-MEE-o

shop
το κατάστημα
to ka-TA-stee-ma

station
ο σταθμός
o sta-THMOS

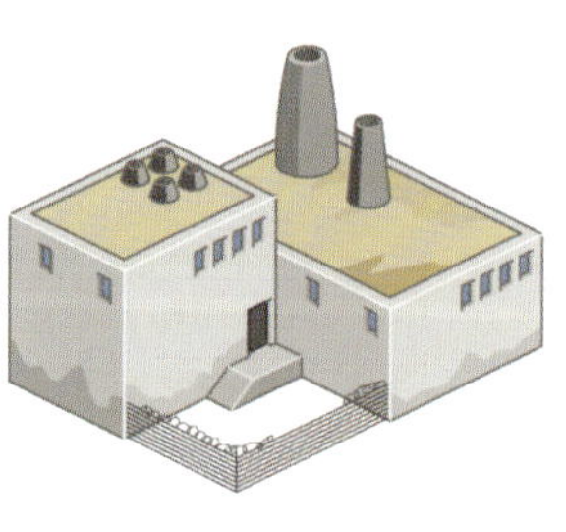

factory
το εργοστάσιο
to er-go-STA-see-o

market
η αγορά
ee a-go-RA

cinema
ο κινηματογράφος
o kee-nee-ma-to-GRA-fos

church
η εκκλησία
ee e-klee-SEE-a

The street - Ο δρόμος

ο DRO-mos

sidewalk
το πεζοδρόμιο
to pe-zo-DRO-mee-o

street
ο δρόμος
o DRO-mos

bus stop
η στάση λεωφορείου
ee STA-see le-o-fo-REE-oo

crosswalk
η διάβαση πεζών
e dee-A-va-see pe-ZON

traffic light
το φανάρι
to fa-NA-ree

highway
ο αυτοκινητόδρομος
o af-to-kee-nee-TO-dro-mos

road signs
τα σήματα
ta SEE-ma-ta

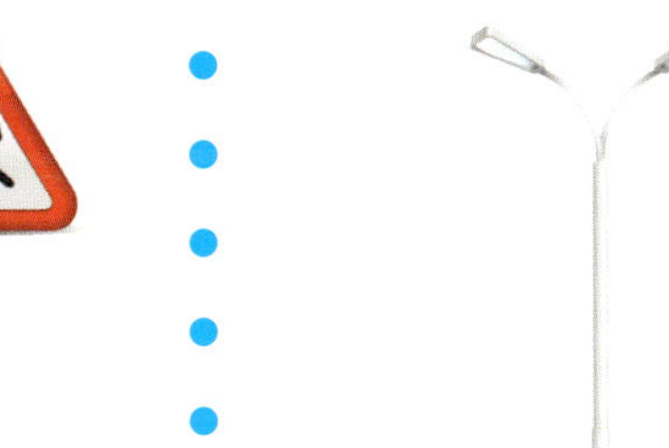

streetlight
τα φώτα του δρόμου
ta FO-ta too DRO-moo

police officer
ο αστυνομικός
o a-stee-no-mee-KOS

Vehicles - Τα οχήματα

ta o-HEE-ma-ta

bus
το λεωφορείο
to le-o-fo-REE-o

car
το αυτοκίνητο
to af-to-KEE-nee-to

bicycle
το ποδήλατο
to po-DEE-la-to

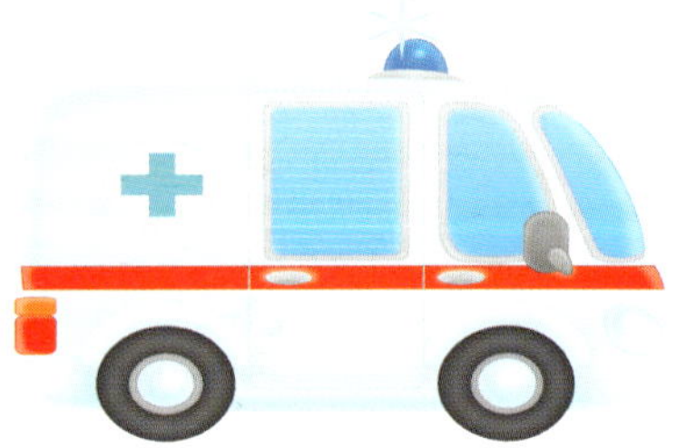

ambulance
το ασθενοφόρο
to as-the-no-FO-ro

police car
το περιπολικό
to pe-ri-po-lee-KO

motorcycle
η μοτοσικλέτα
ee mo-to-see-KLE-ta

school bus
το σχολικό λεωφορείο
to s(h)o-lee-KO le-o-fo-REE-o

fire engine
το πυροσβεστικό όχημα
to pee-ro-sve-stee-KO O-hee-ma

truck
το φορτηγό
to for-tee-GO

The park - Το πάρκο

to PAR-ko

merry-go-round
γύρω-γύρω όλοι
YEE-ro-YEE-ro O-lee

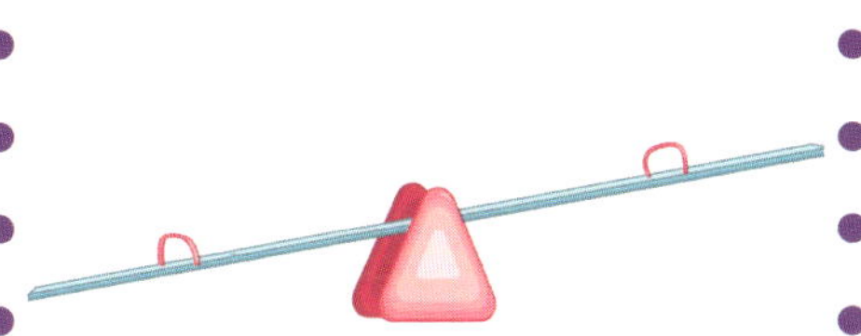

seesaw
η τραμπάλα
ee tra-BA-la

swing
η κούνια
ee KOO-nya

girl
το κορίτσι
to ko-REE-tsee

boy
το αγόρι
to a-GO-ree

lake
η λίμνη
ee LEE-mnee

bench
το παγκάκι
to pa-GA-kee

kite
ο χαρταετός
o har-ta-e-TOS

path
το μονοπάτι
to mo-no-PA-tee

The hospital - Το νοσοκομείο

to no-so-ko-MEE-o

doctor
ο γιατρός
o ya-TROS

nurse
η νοσοκόμα
ee no-so-KO-ma

x-ray
η ακτινογραφία
ee a-ktee-no-gra-FEE-

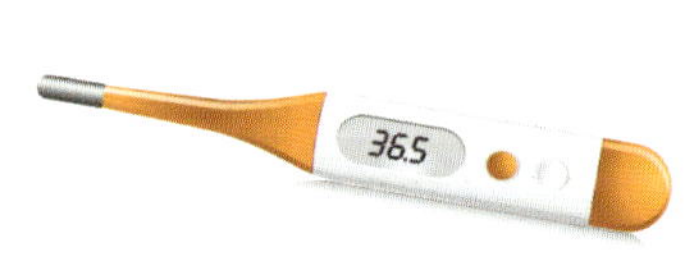

thermometer
το θερμόμετρο
to ther-MO-me-tro

bandage
ο επίδεσμος
o e-PEE-des-mos

crutches
οι πατερίτσες
ee pa-ter-EE-tses

wheel chair
το αναπηρικό καροτσάκι
to a-na-pee-ree-KO ka-ro-TSA-kee

medicine
το φάρμακο
to FAR-ma-ko

cast
ο γύψος
o YEE-psos

The supermarket - Το παντοπωλείο

to pan-to-po-LEE-o

egg
το αβγό
to av-GO

bread
το ψωμί
to pso-MEE

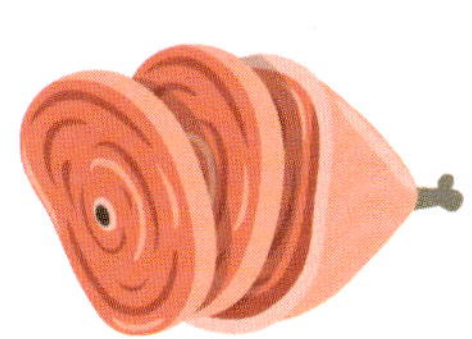

meat
το κρέας
to KRE-as

sugar
η ζάχαρη
ee ZA-ha-ree

milk
το γάλα
to GA-la

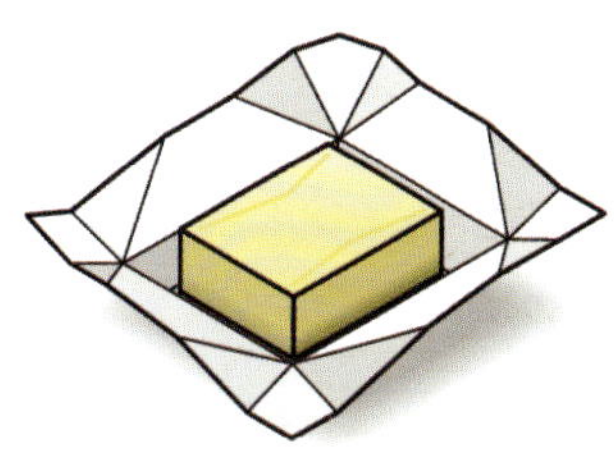

butter
το βούτυρο
to VOO-tee-ro

pasta
τα μακαρόνια
ta ma-ka-RO-nya

fish
το ψάρι
to PSA-ree

rice
το ρύζι
to REE-zee

Fruit - Τα φρούτα

ta FROO-ta

apple
το μήλο
to MEE-lo

orange
το πορτοκάλι
to por-to-KA-lee

cherry
το κεράσι
to ke-RA-see

grapes
τα σταφύλια
ta sta-FEE-lya

watermelon
το καρπούζι
to kar-POO-zee

banana
η μπανάνα
ee ba-NA-na

pomegranate
το ρόδι
to RO-dee

pear
το αχλάδι
to ah-LA-dee

strawberry
η φράουλα
ee FRA-oo-la

Vegetables - Τα λαχανικά

ta la-ha-nee-KA

potato
η πατάτα
ee pa-TA-ta

onion
το κρεμμύδι
to kre-MEE-dee

tomato
η ντομάτα
ee do-MA-ta

carrot
το καρότο
to ka-RO-to

broccoli
το μπρόκολο
to BRO-ko-lo

eggplant
η μελιτζάνα
ee me-lee-TZA-na

cucumber
το αγγούρι
to a-GOO-ree

pepper
η πιπεριά
ee pee-per-YA

corn
το καλαμπόκι
to ka-lam-BO-kee

The country - Η εξοχή

ee e-kso-HEE

tree
το δέντρο
to DEN-dro

grass
το γρασίδι
to gra-SEE-dee

flower
το λουλούδι
to loo-LOO-dee

field
το χωράφι
to ho-RA-fee

bird
το πουλί
to poo-LEE

bridge
η γέφυρα
ee YE-fee-ra

forest
το δάσος
to DA-sos

river
το ποτάμι
to po-TA-mee

mountain
το βουνό
to voo-NO

Forest animals - Τα ζώα του δάσους

ta ZO-a too DA-soos

fox
η αλεπού
ee a-le-POO

deer
το ελάφι
to e-LA-fee

rabbit
ο λαγός
o la-GOS

squirrel
ο σκίουρος
o SKEE-oo-ros

butterfly
η πεταλούδα
ee pe-ta-LOO-da

bear
η αρκούδα
ee ar-KOO-da

beetle
το σκαθάρι
to ska-THA-ree

caterpillar
η κάμπια
ee KAM-bya

fly
η μύγα
ee MEE-ga

The farm - Το αγρόκτημα

to a-GRO-ktee-ma

rooster
ο κόκορας
o KO-ko-ras

horse
το άλογο
to A-lo-go

cow
η αγελάδα
ee a-ye-LA-da

cat
η γάτα
ee GA-ta

duck
η πάπια
ee PA-pya

pig
το γουρούνι
to goo-ROO-nee

dog
ο σκύλος
o SKEE-los

sheep
το πρόβατο
to PRO-va-to

goat
η κατσίκα
ee ka-TSEE-ka

Baby animals - Τα μικρά ζώα

ta mee-KRA ZO-a

chick
το κοτοπουλάκι
to ko-to-poo-LA-kee

foal
το πουλάρι
to poo-LA-ree

calf
το μοσχαράκι
to mo-(s)ha-RA-kee

kitten
το γατάκι
to ga-TA-kee

duckling
το παπάκι
to pa-PA-kee

piglet
το γουρουνάκι
to goo-roo-NA-kee

puppy
το σκυλάκι
to skee-LA-kee

lamb
το αρνάκι
to ar-NA-kee

kid
το κατσικάκι
to ka-tsee-KA-kee

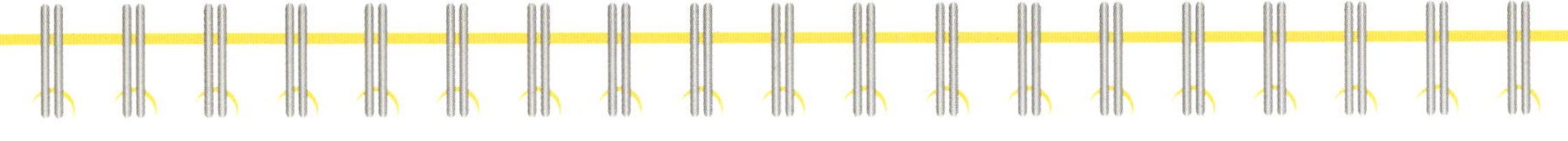

At the beach - Στην παραλία

steen pa-ra-LEE-a

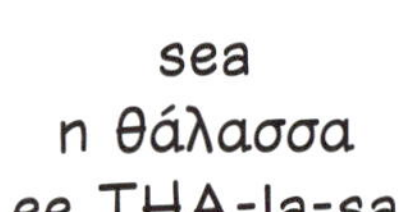

sea
η θάλασσα
ee THA-la-sa

waves
τα κύματα
ta KEE-ma-ta

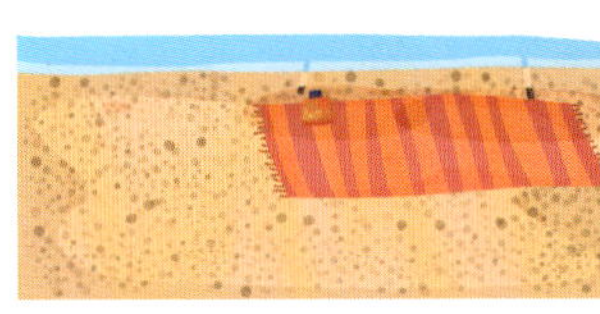

sand
η άμμος
ee A-mos

umbrella
η ομπρέλα θαλάσσης
ee om-BRE-la tha-LA-sees

bucket
το κουβαδάκι
to koo-va-DA-kee

shell
το κοχύλι
to ko-HEE-lee

seagull
ο γλάρος
o GLA-ros

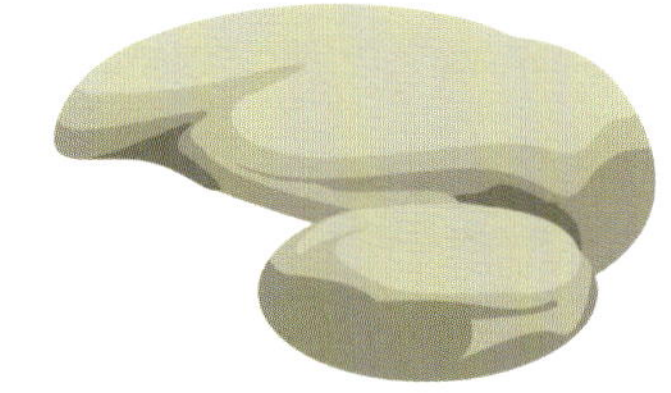

rock
ο βράχος
o VRA-hos

boat
η βάρκα
ee VAR-ka

Under the sea - Κάτω από τη θάλασσα

KA-to a-PO tee THA-la-sa

seabed
ο βυθός
o vee-THOS

fish
το ψάρι
to PSA-ree

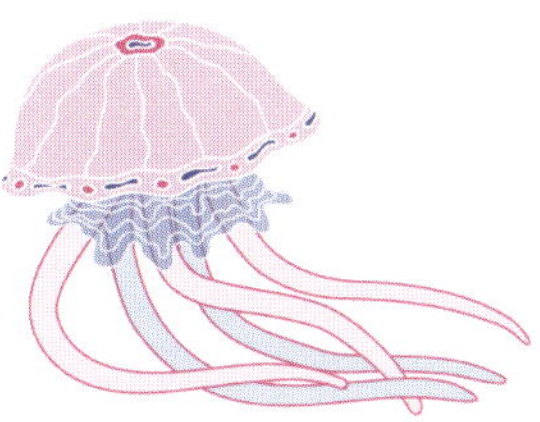

jellyfish
η τσούχτρα
ee TSOO-htra

crab
το καβούρι
to ka-VOO-ree

diver
ο δύτης
o DEE-tees

seaweed
τα φύκια
ta FEE-kya

shark
ο καρχαρίας
o kar-ha-REE-as

octopus
το χταπόδι
to hta-PO-dee

starfish
ο αστερίας
o as-ter-EE-as

The zoo - Ο ζωολογικός κήπος

o Zo-o-lo-gee-KOS KEE-pos

lion
το λιοντάρι
to lyon-DA-ree

panda
το πάντα
to PAN-da

snake
το φίδι
to FEE-dee

tiger
η τίγρη
ee TEE-gree

elephant
ο ελέφαντας
o e-LE-fan-das

ostrich
η στρουθοκάμηλος
ee stroo-tho-KA-mee-lo

penguin
ο πιγκουίνος
o pee-GWEE-nos

crocodile
ο κροκόδειλος
o kro-KO-dee-los

monkey
η μαϊμού
ee ma-ee-MOO

Toys - Παιχνίδια

ta pe-HNEE-dya

ball
η μπάλα
ee BA-la

water colors
οι νερομπογιές
ee ne-ro-bo-YES

doll
η κούκλα
ee KOO-kla

car
το αυτοκινητάκι
af-to-kee-nee-TA-kee

teddy bear
το αρκουδάκι
to ar-koo-DA-kee

robot
το ρομπότ
to ro-BOT

puzzle
το παζλ
to PA-zle

board game
επιτραπέζιο
e-pee-tra-PEZ-yio

jumping rope
το σχοινάκι
to s(h)ee-NA-kee

The party - Το πάρτι

to PAR-tee

refreshment drink
το αναψυκτικό
to a-na-psee-ktee-KO

birthday cake
η τούρτα
ee TOOR-ta

sandwich
το τοστ
to TOST

sweet
το γλυκό
to glee-KO

cookies
τα μπισκότα
ta bee-SKO-ta

orange juice
η πορτοκαλάδα
ee por-to-ka-LA-da

pizza
η πίτσα
ee PEE-tsa

french fries
οι πατάτες τηγανητές
ee pa-TA-tes tee-gan-ee-TES

ice cream
το παγωτό
to pa-go-TO

The classroom - Η τάξη

ee TA-ksee

classroom
η σχολική αίθουσα
s(h)o-lee-KEE E-thoo-sa

teacher
η δασκάλα
ee da-SKA-la

students
οι μαθητές
ee ma-thee-TES

book
το βιβλίο
to vee-VLEE-o

backpack
η σχολική τσάντα
ee s(h)o-lee-KEE TSAN-da

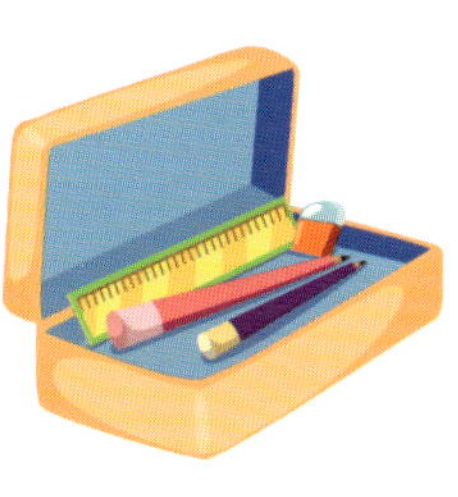

pencil case
η κασετίνα
ee ka-se-TEE-na

pencil
το μολύβι
to mo-LEE-vee

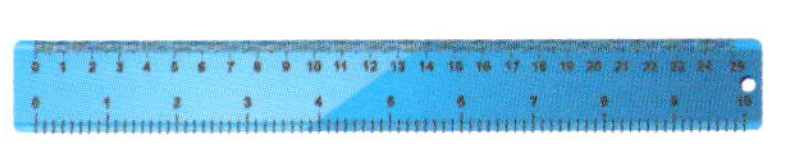

ruler
ο χάρακας
o HA-ra-kas

pen
το στιλό
to stee-LO

Sports - Τα αθλήματα

τα a-THLEE-ma-ta

soccer
το ποδόσφαιρο
to po-DO-sfe-ro

basketball
το μπάσκετ
to BA-sket

volleyball
το βόλεϊ
to VO-le-ee

jogging
το τρέξιμο
to TRE-ksee-mo

swimming
το κολύμπι
to ko-LEEM-bee

gymnastics
η γυμναστική
ee yee-mna-stee-KEE

cycling
το ποδήλατο
to po-DEE-la-to

skiing
το σκι
to SKEE

dancing
ο χορός
o ho-ROS

The weather - Ο καιρός

ο ke-ROS

sun
ο ήλιος
ο EE-lyos

rain
η βροχή
ee vro-HEE

heat
η ζέστη
ee ZES-tee

cloud
το σύννεφο
to SEE-ne-fo

storm
η καταιγίδα
ee ka-te-YEE-da

snow
το χιόνι
to HYO-nee

wind
ο αέρας
ο a-E-ras

fog
η ομίχλη
ee o-MEE-hlee

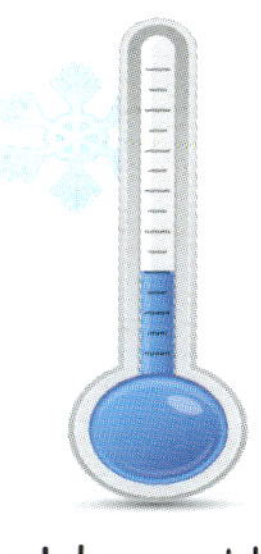

cold weather
το κρύο
to KREE-o

Actions - Κινήσεις
kee-NEE-sees

to walk
περπατώ
per-pa-TO

to stand
στέκομαι
STE-ko-me

to run
τρέχω
TRE-ho

to push
σπρώχνω
SPRO-hno

to hug
αγκαλιάζω
a-ga-LYA-zo

to sit
κάθομαι
KA-tho-me

to pull
τραβώ
tra-VO

to jump
πηδώ
pee-DO

to carry
κουβαλώ
koo-va-LO

Fairy tale words - Λέξεις από τα παραμύθια

LE-ksees a-PO ta pa-ra-MEE-thya

castle
το κάστρο
to KA-stro

dragon
ο δράκος
o DRA-kos

fairy
η νεράιδα
ee ne-RA-ee-da

prince
ο πρίγκιπας
o PREE-gee-pas

princess
η πριγκίπισσα
ee pri-GEE-pee-sa

mermaid
η γοργόνα
ee gor-GO-na

pirate
ο πειρατής
o pee-ra-TEES

witch
η μάγισσα
ee MA-gee-sa

knight
ο ιππότης
o ee-PO-tees

Tools - Τα εργαλεία

ta er-ga-LEE-a

wheelbarrow
το καροτσάκι
to ka-ro-TSA-kee

wrench
το γαλλικό κλειδί
to ga-lee-KO klee-DEE

hammer
το σφυρί
to sfee-REE

nail
το καρφί
to kar-FEE

paintbrush
το πινέλο
to pee-NE-lo

shovel
το φτυάρι
to FTYA-ree

screwdriver
το κατσαβίδι
to ka-tsa-VEE-dee

measuring tape
η μεζούρα
ee me-ZOO-ra

saw
το πριόνι
to pree-O-nee

The construction site - Η οικοδομή

ee ee-ko-do-MEE

crane
ο γερανός
o ye-ra-NOS

cement mixer
η μπετονιέρα
ee be-to-NYE-ra

dump truck
το φορτηγό
to for-tee-GO

digger
ο εκσκαφέας
o ek-ska-FE-as

construction worker
ο οικοδόμος
o ee-ko-DO-mos

construction site
η οικοδομή
ee ee-ko-do-MEE

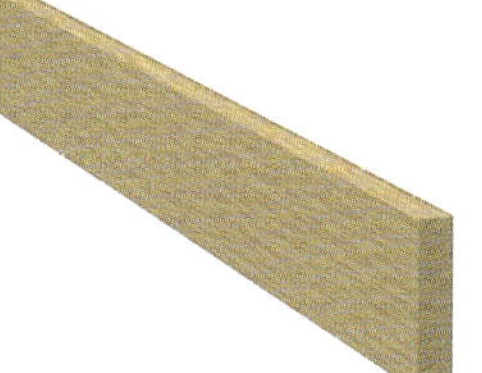

wood
το ξύλο
to KSEE-lo

brick
το τούβλο
to TOO-vlo

ladder
η σκάλα
ee SKA-la

Luggage - Οι αποσκευές

ee a-po-ske-VES

suitcase
η βαλίτσα
ee va-LEE-tsa

briefcase
ο χαρτοφύλακας
o har-to-FEE-la-kas

backpack
το σακίδιο
to sa-KEE-dee-yo

basket
το καλάθι
to ka-LA-thee

shopping bag
η σακούλα
ee sa-KOO-la

laptop case
η τσάντα υπολογιστή
ee TSAN-da ee-po-lo-gee-S

trunk
το μπαούλο
to ba-OO-lo

wallet
το πορτοφόλι
to por-to-FO-lee

handbag
η τσάντα
ee TSAN-da

Train travel - Το ταξίδι με το τρένο

to ta-KSEE-dee me to TRE-no

train
το τρένο
to TRE-no

ticket
το εισιτήριο
to ee-see-TEE-ree-o

platform
η αποβάθρα
ee a-po-VA-thra

engineer
ο μηχανικός
o mee-ha-nee-KOS

conductor
ο ελεγκτής
o e-le-GTEES

train station
ο σιδηροδρομικός σταθμός
o see-thee-ro-dro-mee-KOS sta-THMOS

rails
ο σιδηρόδρομος
see-thee-RO-dro-mos

signal
ο σηματοδότης
o see-ma-to-DO-tees

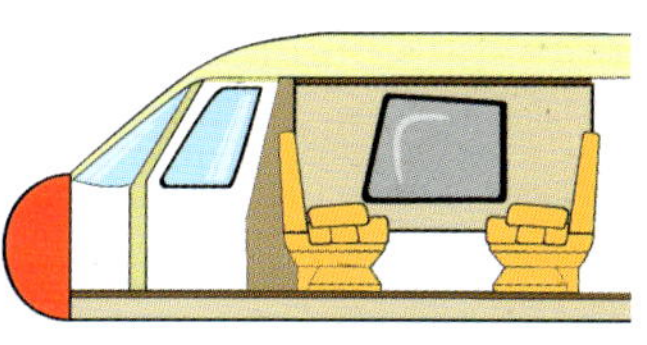

seats
τα καθίσματα
ta ka-THEE-sma-ta

Air travel - Το αεροπορικό ταξίδι

to a-er-ro-po-ree-KO ta-KSEE-dee

airplane
το αεροπλάνο
to a-e-ro-PLA-no

airport
το αεροδρόμιο
to a-e-ro-DRO-mee-o

waiting room
η αίθουσα αναμονής
ee E-thoo-sa a-na-mo-NE

pilot
ο πιλότος
o pee-LO-tos

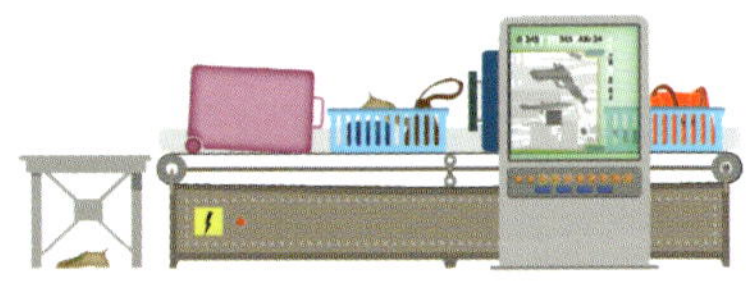

x-ray machine
το μηχάνημα ελέγχου αποσκευών
to mee-HA-nee-ma
e-LE-hoo a-po-ske-VON

cart
το καρότσι
to ka-RO-tsee

stewardess
η αεροσυνοδός
ee a-e-ro-see-no-DOS

seatbelt
η ζώνη ασφαλείας
ee ZO-nee as-fa-LEE-as

passport
το διαβατήριο
to dya-va-TEE-ree-o

At sea - Στη θάλασσα

stee THA-la-sa

yacht
το κότερο
to KO-te-ro

fishing boat
το ψαροκάικο
to psa-ro-KA-ee-ko

rowboat
η βάρκα με κουπιά
ee VAR-ka me koo-PYA

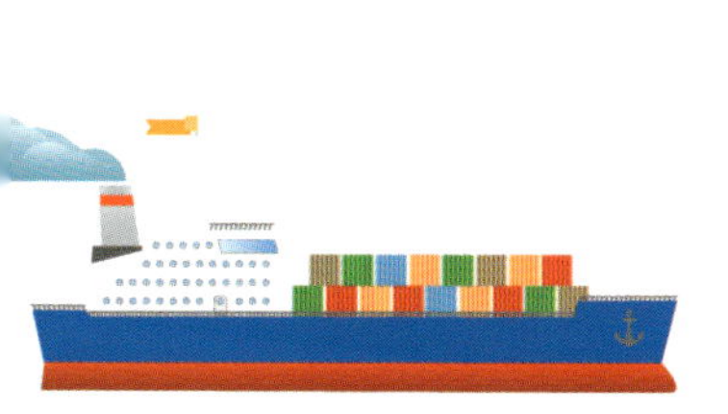

ship
το πλοίο
to PLEE-o

sailing boat
το ιστιοφόρο
to ees-tee-o-FO-ro

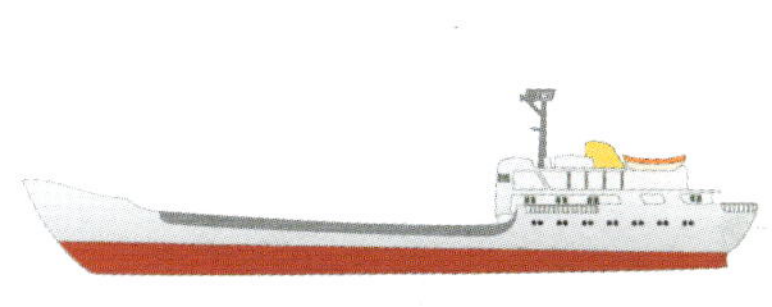

ferry boat
το οχηματαγωγό
to o-hee-ma-ta-go-GO

lighthouse
ο φάρος
o FA-ros

anchor
η άγκυρα
ee A-gee-ra

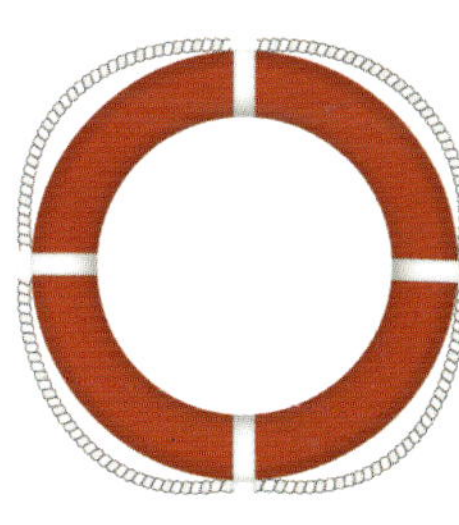

lifesaver
το σωσίβιο
to so-SEE-vee-o

Opposites - Τα αντίθετα

ta an-DEE-the-ta

fat
ο χοντρός/η χοντρή
o hon-DROS/ee hon-DREE

thin
ο λεπτός/η λεπτή
o lep-TOS/ee lep-TEE

ugly
ο άσχημος/η άσχημη
o AS-hee-mos/ee AS-hee-mee

beautiful
ο όμορφος/η όμορφη
o O-mor-fos/ee O-mor-fee

tall
ο ψηλός/η ψηλή
o psee-LOS/ee psee-LEE

short
ο κοντός/η κοντή
o kon-DOS/ee kon-DEE

Opposites - Τα αντίθετα

ta an-DEE-the-ta

slow
ο αργός/η αργή
o ar-GOS/ee ar-GEE

fast
ο γρήγορος/η γρήγορη
o GREE-go-ros/ee GREE-go-ree

dirty
ο βρόμικος/η βρόμικη
o VRO-mee-kos/ee VRO-mee-kee

clean
ο καθαρός/η καθαρή
o ka-tha-ROS/ee ka-tha-REE

sad
ο λυπημένος/η λυπημένη
o lee-pee-ME-nos/ee lee-pee-ME-nee

happy
ο χαρούμενος/η χαρούμενη
o ha-ROO-me-nos/ee ha-ROO-me-nee

Phrases - Εκφράσεις

ek-FRA-sees

How are you?
Τι κάνεις;
TEE KA-nees?

I' m fine.
Είμαι καλά.
EE-me ka-LA.

Good morning.
Καλημέρα.
Ka-lee-ME-ra.

Good afternoon.
Καλησπέρα.
Ka-lee-SPE-ra.

Good evening.
Καλό βράδυ.
Ka-LO VRA-dee.

Good night.
Καληνύχτα.
Ka-lee-NEE-hta.

What is your name?
Πώς σε λένε;
POS se-LE-ne?

My name is Helen.
Με λένε Ελένη.
ME LE-ne e-LE-nee.

How old are you?
Πόσων χρονών είσαι;
PO-son hro-NON EE-se?

I am six years old.
Είμαι έξι χρονών.
EE-me E-ksee hro-NON.

What time is it please?
Τι ώρα είναι παρακαλώ
TEE O-ra EE-ne
pa-ra-ka-LO?

It's seven o 'clock.
Είναι επτά.
EE-ne e-PTA.

Where is the bread?
Πού είναι το ψωμί;
POO EE-ne to pso-MEE?

It is on the table.
Είναι πάνω στο τραπέζι.
EE-ne PA-no sto
tra-PE-zee.

Thank you very much.
Ευχαριστώ πολύ.
Ef-ha-ree-STO po-LEE.

I would like a glass of
water please.
Θέλω ένα ποτήρι νερό
παρακαλώ.
THE-lo E-na po-TEE-re
ne-RO pa-ra-ka-LO.

Phrases - Εκφράσεις

ek-FRA-sees

I like playing ball.
Μου αρέσει να παίζω μπάλα.
\OO a-RE-see na PE-zo BA-la.

I like music very much.
Μου αρέσει πολύ η μουσική.
MOO a-RE-see po-LEE ee moo-see-KEE.

I like pasta very much.
Μου αρέσουν πολύ τα μακαρόνια.
MOO a-RE-soon po-LEE ta ma-ka-RO-nya.

Enjoy your meal!
Καλή όρεξη!
ka-LEE O-re-ksee!

Have a safe trip.
Καλό ταξίδι!
ka-LO ta-KSEE-dee.

Have a good month.
Καλό μήνα.
ka-LO MEE-na.

Merry Christmas!
Καλά Χριστούγεννα!
a-LA hree-STOO-ye-na!

Happy Easter!
Καλό Πάσχα!
ka-LO PAS-ha!

Happy Birthday!
Χρόνια Πολλά!
HRO-nya po-LA!

I love you very much.
Σ' αγαπώ πολύ.
sa-ga-PO po-LEE.

English/αγγλικά - Greek/ελληνικά

airplane το αεροπλάνο.........38
airport το αεροδρόμιο.........38
alarm clock το ξυπνητήρι 7
ambulance το ασθενοφόρο.....14
anchor η άγκυρα.................39
apple το μήλο.....................18
arm το μπράτσο..................10
armchair η πολυθρόνα..........6
aunt η θεία........................4
backpack το σακίδιο...... 29, 36
ball η μπάλα.......................27
banana η μπανάνα...............18
bandage ο επίδεσμος............16
basket το καλάθι..................36
basketball το μπάσκετ 30
bathroom το μπάνιο..............5
bathtub η μπανιέρα..............8
bear η αρκούδα 21
beautiful ο όμορφος/η όμορφη....40
bed το κρεβάτι 7
bedroom το υπνοδωμάτιο......5
beetle το σκαθάρι 21
bench το παγκάκι..................15
bicycle το ποδήλατο........14, 30
bird το πουλί.......................20
birthday cake η τούρτα............28
board game το επιτραπέζιο.........27
boat η βάρκα 24
book το βιβλίο.....................29
boy το αγόρι.........................15
bread το ψωμί 17
brick το τούβλο....................35
bridge η γέφυρα 20
briefcase ο χαρτοφύλακας....36
broccoli το μπρόκολο 19
brother ο αδερφός...............4
bucket το κουβαδάκι............24
bus το λεωφορείο 14
bus stop η στάση λεωφορείου ...13
butter το βούτυρο................17
butterfly η πεταλούδα 21
calf το μοσχαράκι 23
car το αυτοκίνητο..........14, 27
carrot το καρότο..................19
cart το καρότσι....................38
cast ο γύψος.......................16
castle το κάστρο 33
cat η γάτα...........................22
caterpillar η κάμπια.............21
ceiling το ταβάνι..................5
cement mixer η μπετονιέρα..35
cherry το κεράσι 18
chest of drawers το κομοδίνο 7
chick το κοτοπουλάκι...........23
chips οι πατάτες τηγανητές..28
church η εκκλησία 12
cinema ο κινηματογράφος.....12
classroom η σχολική αίθουσα 29
clean ο καθαρός/η καθαρή....41
clothes τα ρούχα 11
cloud το σύννεφο 31
coat το παλτό 11
cold weather το κρύο..........31
comb η χτένα 7
computer ο υπολογιστής.......6
conductor ο ελεγκτής 37
construction site η οικοδομή 35
construction worker ο οικοδόμος 35
cookies τα μπισκότα 28
corn το καλαμπόκι 19
cousins τα ξαδέρφια 4
cow η αγελάδα.....................22
crab το καβούρι 25
crane ο γερανός 35
crocodile ο κροκόδειλος 26
crosswalk η διάβαση πεζών ..13
crutches οι πατερίτσες 16
cucumber το αγγούρι...........19
curtains οι κουρτίνες...........6
cushion το μαξιλαράκι.........6
cycling το ποδήλατο.............30
dad ο μπαμπάς 4
dancing ο χορός 30
deer το ελάφι 21
digger ο εκσκαφέας 35
dirty ο βρόμικος/η βρόμικη...41
diver ο δύτης 25
doctor ο γιατρός 16
dog ο σκύλος........................22
doll η κούκλα 27
door η πόρτα 7
dragon ο δράκος....................33
dress το φόρεμα....................11
duck η πάπια........................22
duckling το παπάκι 23
dump truck το φορτηγό.........35
egg το αβγό 17
eggplant η μελιτζάνα 19
elephant ο ελέφαντας............26
engineer ο μηχανικός 37
eyes τα μάτια 10
factory το εργοστάσιο..........12
fairy η νεράιδα....................33
fast ο γρήγορος/η γρήγορη...41
fat ο χοντρός/η χοντρή 40
father ο πατέρας.................4
ferry boat το οχηματαγωγό ..39
field το χωράφι...................20
fire engine το πυροσβεστικό όχημα.14
fish το ψάρι 17, 25
fishing boat το ψαροκάικο....39
floor το πάτωμα 5
flower το λουλούδι 20
fly η μύγα 21
foal το πουλάρι....................23
fog η ομίχλη........................31
fork το πιρούνι.....................9
forest το δάσος....................20
fox η αλεπού 21
french fries οι πατάτες τηγανητές.28
garden ο κήπος 5
girl το κορίτσι 15
glass το ποτήρι 9
goat η κατσίκα.....................22
grandfather ο παππούς 4
grandmother η γιαγιά..........4
grapes τα σταφύλια..............18
grass το γρασίδι 20
gymnastics η γυμναστική......30
hammer το σφυρί 34
hand το χέρι 10
handbag η τσάντα...............36
happy ο χαρούμενος/η χαρούμενη.....41
hat το καπέλο 11
head το κεφάλι....................10
heat η ζέστη 31
highway ο αυτοκινητόδρομος.13
horse το άλογο 22
house το σπίτι 12
ice cream το παγωτό.............28
jellyfish η τσούχτρα 25
jogging το τρέξιμο 30
jumping rope το σκοινάκι......27
kid το κατσικάκι...................23
kitchen η κουζίνα 5
kite ο χαρταετός 15
kitten το γατάκι....................23
knee το γόνατο....................10
knife το μαχαίρι....................9
knight ο ιππότης 33

Greek/ελληνικά - English/αγγλικά